T0064367

Engaging with local justice issues

regenerateuk.co.uk

iUniverse, Inc.
Bloomington

Contents

Preface

I once heard someone say that God builds his Kingdom on relationships, and from my experience I'm sure that must be true.

I grew up in church – doing, living and breathing church stuff – and most of it very good stuff.

But City Lights started differently for me – it wasn't just about doing something or responding to a need – it was a natural expression, an overflow of a very special friendship.

Mari and I became friends in an unusual way. We discovered almost by 'accident' that God was speaking the very same thing to us about some of the needs in our city. Our friendship was formed as we talked over coffee about the troubles we saw and our confidence that God could fix things. Our growing friendship gave us the courage to start doing something about it.

One thing led to another and we found ourselves key players in a residential set-up for vulnerable young girls. We began to invite other friends into the story.

The experience was exciting and also strangely mundane. On one hand we were collecting dramatic tear-jerking stories, and on the other hand, most of our time was spent serving in very everyday ways. It was in one of those normal moments, when we were hanging up laundry, that Mari and I started to dream.

We imagined the people and churches we knew in our city connected in very real practical ways to the needs in our city. We were in contact with a lot of under-resourced projects and people who worked in areas of great need, and it seemed like a fun idea to connect the dots - connect the needs with those who were eager to help. That's really what it was... just a fun idea between friends, while we were hanging out the laundry.

It could have very easily just stayed an idea, because most of the time that is what happens with ideas: they just stay ideas. But because it was a shared idea between friends we had the courage to give it a go. We figured that we didn't have much to lose. We could just set up some initiatives for our friends one weekend and see what happened.

But ideas between friends have a way of snowballing and the response was more than we had expected. Forty people showed up to the little meeting we had to pitch the idea – some we didn't even know! Before we knew it, we had enough projects to fill a week and more than 100 volunteers to get the job done. And that was how City Lights was born. An idea between friends. God building his Kingdom in a very exceptional-ordinary way.

Erin Lucas
Co-Founder of City Lights New Zealand
www.citylights.org.nz

Introduction

The City Lights Vision: City Lights creates pathways for groups and individuals to engage with local justice issues.

You are holding a collection of stories. The aim of this collection is to equip and inspire you to make a positive impact in your own community through relationships and creative initiatives.

In this book, you will read about Dave and Will, who developed gardens on wasteland in inner city London council estates, encouraging residents to be part of the process of renewal and creativity by growing plants and vegetables. Will hosts community harvest feasts, bringing together local residents to eat their own locally-grown produce. Andy, while he was in his twenties, started a lunch club for isolated elderly people, rallying his student friends to help serve homemade meals in a borrowed church hall. Pauline responded to a news bulletin about the lack of housing for refugees and asylum seekers by setting up homes across North London to provide safe housing. Annie set up regular meals in her church building for homeless people and rough sleepers. Mark started a football club for local lads from an estate in London, most of whom were from extremely difficult backgrounds and not in education or employment. Countless others have weeded gardens for families referred by social services, mentored children in foster care and painted walls in refuges. Abroad, Mick and Ruby moved into an inner city slum community in the heart of Manilla for nine years with their young children.

At the heart of City Lights are stories and friendships. Behind every idea, initiative or 'project,' is the desire to build meaningful relationship. Every story and contribution in this book points to the importance of this one foundation: true, authentic relationship!

We hope these stories will inspire you to step out of the familiar and engage with people and needs in your setting. We hope these stories will empower you to discover pathways into your own community, listen and respond to the needs around you, build relationships and process the difficult questions and challenges you will encounter along the way.

Mari Day-Revell
Co-Founder of City Lights

Learning to Love Well

Debs Hunt

Debs currently lives in Vancouver where she is studying for her Masters in Theology at Regent College. Prior to moving to Canada, Debs lived with friends on a council estate in Battersea, London where she spent time exploring what it means to love her neighbour and practice resurrection within her community. She also worked in micro-finance in London, helping those who are excluded in society become included with their dignity restored through self-employment.

City Lights Intro

The piece you are about to read calls us to shift our focus away from projects, numbers and programmes, towards friendships. This might challenge our thinking, our priorities, the way we spend our time or our definition of success.

Projects and programmes can be good but friendships are invaluable. As Debs discovered: "The only way to deep and lasting transformation was through friendship – friendship with God and friendship with others"

A s I began to read about Jesus in the gospels, I noticed that he had an incredibly unusual way of living. I was struck by how Jesus lived alongside the poor and marginalised. For him, they weren't a 'project', they were his friends. Jesus moved beyond his cultural and social norms to befriend those found on the margins his society.

I found Jesus' social circle deeply challenging. His friends were the outcasts and sinners in society. My friends, by contrast, were pretty similar to me – privileged, middle class and educated. He spent time at the periphery: tax collectors' homes, in the street with prostitutes, alone in the desert. By contrast, I had just completed a degree at a prestigious university, the world was at my fingertips with career opportunities and places to travel. I moved to London, and following a year-long internship with The Besom, a ministry that aims to bridge the gap between the rich and the poor, I asked God where he wanted me to live. In response, God provided not so much an answer but a new motivation for my question: 'I want you to simply love people back to life.' God didn't tell me to move overseas, to begin projects (although projects can be good) or to begin a charity (though charities can be good). God asked me to love people back to life.

In an attempt to break out of my middle-class, privileged-but-often-slightly-dull, homogenous bubble, some friends and I moved into the ninth floor of a block of flats on a Battersea council estate. Here we grappled with the command to practise resurrection love amidst the deadening effects of unemployment, the dehumanising welfare system, and the allure of addiction, which whispered attractive but undeliverable promises. Mother Teresa's words came to reverberate in my ears: "the greatest form of poverty is loneliness."

In my naivety, I thought many people's lives would change. I imagined a re-enactment of Ezekiel in the valley of dry bones (Ez.37.1-14), each bone simultaneously coming alive and a large, fleshly army assembling.

I was sorely mistaken.

In this chapter we are going to journey together and explore what it means to live out the kingdom of God in our communities. I will tell stories of people's lives, for it has been through story that I have learnt the most: from personal experience or from the experience of others. Some of what I write I have come to know from mistakes I made, people I hurt, or wisdom passed on to me from others. I make no claims to have 'figured it out', and regardless, the beauty of the Spirit is that each situation is profoundly unique. However, I have noticed certain patterns and themes along the way. It is these that I share with the prayer that they will guide you further into the heart of Christ for your neighbours and neighbourhood.

Getting started: Poverty of Place, Richness of Time

Very near the beginning, I learnt one of the most important lessons: 'doing it' was all about friendship. Note that I had to learn this. I started out with a deep desire to 'do' and see radical transformation in people's lives, and I left after five years knowing that the only way to deep and lasting transformation was through friendship – friendship with God and friendship with others.

I expect this simple lesson will take a lifetime to fully realise.

In my experience, getting started is both the hardest and the most straightforward part. Starting out on journey is often the easiest part – energy is high, people are excited, the air is pregnant with endless possibilities and God is big. But however well we start out, it is guaranteed that at some point we hit a roadblock as we ask the question – so now what? I found myself with an SW11 postcode, which wasn't dissimilar to what I was used to, and yet my surroundings felt like I was a million miles away from anything that resembled familiarity. Whether it was the lifts smelling of fresh urine or the eclectic character of my Somali, Irish, Indian, Afro-Caribbean and Geordie neighbours – I was a stranger in a foreign land.

> **The only way to deep and lasting transformation was through friendship – friendship with God and friendship with others.**

I realised that I had brought my frustration of living a busy London life with me – I was living somewhere intentionally, desiring to meet people and to begin to practice resurrection in dead places, and yet I was time poor. This is one of the first roadblocks we come across – our demanding schedules leave us little or no time for our neighbours. We rush in from work and then rush back out again for a dinner party or an evening meeting or a drink at the pub. In those first few months, I became more and more frustrated with the lack of names that we knew. We had moved on to the estate in order to see transformation, but we weren't seeing much of anyone's life at all. I shouldn't have been surprised: we live in a society where we are money rich yet time poor. One of the constant struggles of living in any big city is that we get swept up in the busyness of life. But the reality is that if I say 'yes' to one thing, then that means I am automatically saying 'no' to something else.

Let's face it: life is full, busy, demanding, and we regularly embark upon juggling acts of far too many people and activities. Being busy has become a drug in the Western world. The poet T.S. Eliot understood this temptation as he observed in his Four Quartets "we are distracted from distractions by distractions." How true. Admittedly, we often thrive from being busy, when life consists of a smorgasbord of the 'good' things that give us purpose, make us feel useful and connect us with others. And yet, 'good' things can be the major obstacles that prevent us from seeing the 'great' thing of change within our communities. In our world of immediate gratification and technological multitasking, we esteem efficiency, maximisation and productivity – which we let seep into our mindset of loving God and loving neighbour. Love takes time, cannot be hurried and is extravagantly wasteful.

The economics of the Kingdom are entirely otherworldly.

For me, the answer to this time poverty was to cut my working week to four days, leaving Friday as a day to be intentionally 'available' as a good neighbour. My first Friday – nine am, strong cup of coffee in one hand, bible in the other – I began to pray asking God what it was he would have me do with this long empty day that was full of possibilities. God is often surprising in his answers: 'Do you know how much I love you?' In fact, this was the only answer that I heard all morning. To be honest, I felt rather frustrated that God had decided to belabour the point and felt as though my morning had been wasted. Didn't God want to speak to me about how to go out and love my neighbour? Instead, he seemed to simply tell me how much he loved me, which I thought I already knew.

I went to walk out my frustration in the local park, and as I was returning I met Douglas, my seventy-nine-year-old Sri-Lankan neighbour, returning to his flat after a hospital stay. We began to chat and seeing his heavy luggage, I offered my assistance. This then turned into him asking whether I had any spare time to go the supermarket and buy him a few essentials. For once, time was actually something I had! We ended up spending a couple of hours together that day, drinking tea, and poring over photos of his family as he recounted their journey from Sri-Lanka to Britain thirty years earlier. It was his parting words that struck me most – other than family, no one else had ever been to his flat for a cup of tea.

This day taught me two of the most crucial lessons that helped me live well over the next five years, and for life to come. Firstly, the primary and most essential posture for me was one of prayer and receiving. It was only from a place of deep friendship with God that I was to go to my neighbour. Secondly, what my neighbour needed most was genuine friendship. Both of these required my most costly possession – my time. Again, T.S. Eliot understands this conundrum well: "A condition of absolute simplicity, costing not less than everything." Friendship with God and friendship with neighbour: these are the central tenets needed to transform our communities, and what I learnt as I lived on that Battersea council estate.

Friendship with God

Our intimacy with God is central to 'doing the stuff' within our communities and living authentically missional lives. All too often, this gets glossed over in a flurry of activity 'for God'. This is where we become deeply rooted in Him, the vine. It is the posture of being 'IN CHRIST' not just alongside Him or in consultation with Him, but in a position of absolute dependence on him. This 'in-ness' is the place that we are called to reside, so that the two great myths of mission are destroyed:

Myth 1: 'I can do it on my own'

Myth 2: 'I can do it on my own with God.'

We are created to need both God and others. The key posture is participation – with God and others in His Kingdom. Saint John is adamant about this truth, as he recounts the words of Jesus: "Remain in me and I will remain in you. No branch can bear fruit by itself: it must remain in the vine. Neither can you bear fruit unless you remain in me." (John 15:4) It is as we dwell 'in' Christ that we bear fruit. It is here that we learn to recognise the still small voice, where we are able to rid ourselves of our ideals that so quickly become idols, and instead live by our truest and often most neglected identity as a son or daughter of God. Pause for a moment.

Do either of those two myths resonate with you? If so, in what ways? Examine your posture before God as you live in your community – what word best describes it? Is it 'in-ness', consultation with God, side-by-side alongside God, or something else?

As soon as we allow anything other than our intimacy with Christ to take precedence, we fall prey to idols in our lives. I found that it was only from a place of intimacy with God that I was able to do anything at all. For each person it will be different, for we all relate and nurture our relationship with God in different ways. But it is important that we identify some of the ways that we do this, and allow these to form our mission, rather than our mission defining who we are. The latter way round gives too much room for our identity to be rooted in what we do rather than who we are, in results rather than people, and in the visible rather than the invisible finger-prints of God.

"Do not depend on the hope of results. You may have to face the fact that your work will be apparently worthless and even achieve no result at all, if not perhaps results opposite to what you expect. As you get used to this idea, you start more and more to concentrate not on the results, but on the value, the rightness, the truth of the work itself. You gradually struggle less and less for an idea and more and more for specific people. In the end, it is the reality of personal relationship that saves everything." (Thomas Merton)

This brilliant quote by Merton poses two questions:

Question 1: Are there ways in which your ideals have become your idols?

Question 2: What is your definition of success?

As I attempted to live out love of God and love of neighbour, my definition of 'success' needed to be radically adjusted. My Western, utilitarian, 'tit for tat' mindset needed to be transformed into one that placed obedience to God before obligation to people or results. I was forced to learn to trust more in what was unseen than what was seen. I grew sceptical about anything that produced instant results and began to understand that if something didn't make sense in the eyes of the world, it just might have the mark of God on it. I still saw the validity of programmes, but only when they had their rightful place of being subservient to, and born out of, friendship.

However, I caution you that this can be a lonely place to live in. Some of those around you will be eagerly asking how your estate mission is going. What are you 'doing'? Whose lives are being saved? What programmes are you starting? We have lost the understanding that love takes time, that friendships based on trust are not instantly built, and that much of what we achieve is unquantifiable. I found that I needed to have a few key people around me to encourage me when I was discouraged with questions like these and was asking – 'what on earth am I doing?'

A question to ask: Who are the people that God has placed around me that share a kingdom understanding of success and results that will encourage me in times of discouragement?

Demands of life, the need around us, our mobile phones and social calendars are often such loud voices that we neglect the real life-giving, 'feeding and watering' that we get from intimacy with Christ and living deeply rooted in Him. In reaching out and coming alongside others we can be blind to our own desperate need of friendship with God. It is only as we spend time cultivating this primary relationship that God's life can flow through us to others.

How can I deepen my relationship with God – both individually and corporately?

Friendship with Neighbour

In the Great Commission, Jesus mandated His followers to go out and 'make disciples' of all nations. He does not require us to make converts, but to participate with Him in the process of discipleship. This is inextricably linked with friendship, as Jesus' disciples became His friends. In John's gospel, Jesus is explicit in His desire to move beyond servanthood into friendship. "I no longer call you servants...instead I call you friends." (John 15:15).

It was Susan who taught me that this was about people rather than programmes, discipleship through friendship rather than random-encounter-conversions. I had seen her around the estate for a while: a young mum with two kids, who barely seemed to be coping, and rather spaced-out most of the time. I had felt a sense that I was going to be friends with her, I had prayed regularly for her, and for an opportunity to get to know her. One Friday the opportunity came. We bumped into each other and began chatting. After a while she invited me in for a cup of tea. As I walked into her damp, dark, undecorated home, I began to see how easy it would be to give it a lick of paint and get some decent furniture. In my desire to help, I readily suggested that if she needed decorating, then I would be happy to help. To my utter surprise, she instantly turned hostile, wheeled around from the kettle, and questioned in an accusatory tone: "what are you, a f**king Jehovah's Witness?" Her words hit me hard, as I realised that my arrogance in my own ability and my 'to-do' mentality had steamrollered her self-esteem, demeaned her pride in her home and made her feel like a charity-case. She wanted friendship – I offered her a service.

Jesus' encounter with the Samaritan woman in John 4 radically demonstrates that the Kingdom of God is not about the 'haves' helping the 'have-nots'. Jesus' compassion broke both cultural and gender barriers to address a woman who was stigmatised and marginalised. He engaged with, listened to, empowered, received from, and loved this one woman back to life. The story tells us that Jesus rendered her irrevocably changed. She didn't feel patronised or looked down upon, as I am sure most men had made her feel. Why else was she alone at the well at the hottest time of the day? In her day, water collecting was a social activity that was carried out by women in the cool hours of the morning. Jesus meets her in the heat of the midday sun, piercing stigma and avoidance, and asks her for help.

This is a great story to spend some time with, as well as the Genesis 16 story of Hagar's encounter with the angel at the well. What do you notice about the way in which Jesus speaks with the Samaritan woman and the way the angel of the Lord speaks to the servant Hagar? What do these encounters tell us about friendship?

Sandra became the Samaritan woman in my life. She was my neighbour – a single mother, illiterate, and severely depressed. She had attempted suicide five times. Her depression was fed by her dark, dingy, undecorated flat, a broken bed that she shared with her teenage daughter, and repeated abuse from a previous partner. She existed – but she had never really lived life. She walked around in grave clothes.

Our friendship began after she had mentioned to another neighbour that she was looking for someone to paint her kitchen, but had no money to pay. Some friends and I offered to paint her kitchen, and it was over paint charts and endless cups of coffee, that we began the mammoth job of painting her entire flat. I watched her, cautious and sceptical at first, steeped in shame and embarrassment at her need. Like Ezekiel's army coming back to life, ligament-by-ligament and tendon-by-tendon, Sandra came to trust and confide in us as she picked up a paintbrush and joined in. After some months she began to join us for pizza after an evening of painting. And the end result was a beautiful, nurturing oasis from the trials and rigours of her life. But more than that, Sandra came to call me a friend. The friendship grew.

Sandra's dream was to travel abroad, but she had never owned a passport and had only twice even ventured outside London. And so, three years later, when a friend gave me two free first-class train tickets to Paris, my first thought was of Sandra. After a rushed venture to acquire a passport for her, the two of us went to France to celebrate her birthday, climbing the Eiffel Tower and sailing down the Seine – a day to remember for both of us! Over the five years of friendship with Sandra, I watched change in her life that was slower than a snail's pace (and sometimes a snail going backwards!) but change nonetheless.

As Sandra encountered hope for her life, we watched her give out some of what she had received. It was from the place of friendship that she couldn't fail to become curious about our faith in Jesus and the mark of His love over our lives. She helped organise and run a community bus that provided a place where our neighbours could receive a free manicure, be prayed for, drink coffee, and experience a fraction of the love of God and His kingdom. She wanted to create a space where people could be loved back to life. The bus was part of a dream to foster community, not isolation, and make people feel beautiful in a society wracked with low self-esteem.

Through our friendships with our neighbours like Sandra, we have learned that walking alongside those who are materially poor begins with befriending and loving one person. In loving this one person we are able to witness what Jesus meant when he declared that he came to bring life in its fullness. As we let go of the need to see impressive numbers of people know Jesus, we are miraculously able to move into more authentic friendship with those that are placed in front of us. After five years of living intentionally within my community, I would say I developed friendships with about six women and their families, of which three were regular, deep and intentional. This may not seem like much. However, the more my new friends invited me into their lives, the more I realised that true friendship was about loving the one person in front of me to the best of my capacity. We are all fractured and broken, and we all need to know that someone cares for and values us.

My friendships with my neighbours also showed me that I needed others – it was too much for me alone. It is essential that we have a group around us, or if not a group, then at least one or two others. Jesus sent the disciples out two by two, and almost without exception Jesus took some of his disciples with him wherever he went. Why is this so important? Because we were not made to do it alone. If we try to do it alone, then we get a martyr complex, or even worse a messiah complex, and find ourselves in a dangerously isolated place, with our pride inflated. Naturally, we all have different gifts, and operate as different parts of the body, but this difference is not a licence to lead alone – the 'lone ranger' syndrome. Whether it was carol singing with our neighbours or Christmas corridor parties or painting homes, much of the neighbour-loving we did was as a community of friends desiring to live out the works and words of Jesus. We learnt that small acts of kindness go a long way, whether it was remembering thoughtful details from previous conversations, or recalling names or finding out people's birthdays and writing a card. There are always opportunities to love people well when we have time.

Reflection
Take some time to think about these highlights from the chapter:
My faithfulness is important: my service isn't essential.
The way we live our days is the way we live our life. (Annie Dillard)
Learn to love well.
My interruptions are my ministry. (Thomas Merton)
Learn to do a few things well.
A community that plays together stays together.

Now take some time to consider the following questions:
How do you nurture your friendship with God?
How can you create space to develop and nurture friendships with others?
We all need friendships. Identify people in your own life who energise you, encourage you and challenge you!

Ruby Duncan

Ruby, her husband Mick and three children have lived and worked with local neighbourhoods and churches in NZ, Australia and the Philippines. In Manila, they squatted in a slum and lived very simply. Now based in Auckland New Zealand, Ruby is the CEO of a charity called Iosis, working with families who are caught in patterns of poverty, family violence and addictions, supporting them to make positive changes for the sake of their children.

City Lights Intro

A few years ago I was at a planning weekend for the youth workers at my church. We had been discussing plans for the coming year. I had expressed my ideas on a number of occasions. I believed I was right and every time an alternative idea was offered I repeated what I had already said more and more forcefully. "I think we all know what you think. How about you just listen for a change?!" The rebuke came from one of the older and respected youth workers. I wanted to crawl into a corner. I stopped talking. I was forced to listen, and as I listened I realised something. I was wrong.

Are you a good listener? Would those closest to you agree? What does being a good listener involve? Can you remember a time in your own life when you felt listened to? The piece you are about to read unpacks these questions. It looks at the importance of being a good listener and what it takes to be a good listener.

Go to the people. Live with them. Love them. Start with what they know. Build with what they have. But with the best leaders, when the work is done, the task is accomplished, the people will say 'we have done this ourselves'.
(Lao Tzu)

Listening is the beginning of any relationship. All of us are formed by our own experiences and view of truth and the world. From the place where we sit and see the world, we come to our conclusions and beliefs about what we imagine others are experiencing. These lead on to assumptions about what we believe others will need or want.

> **If truly listening we must always be prepared to change our minds, even on the most deeply held and treasured beliefs**

The challenge is to wipe our own mind of these assumptions when we come to listen. If we cannot do this, we will continue to hear and sift through this filter. We will automatically misinterpret what others are saying.

We must also remember as we come to listen, that others will not tell us the whole story at the beginning of our relationship. They will not know if we are ready to listen, and will naturally assume that we have come with our own agenda. Many have learnt to manipulate the agenda of others, and put forward what they imagine others want to hear. This means that listening is not a one-off, or short-term, event. Listening is forever and will lead us to constantly readjust and examine our own thoughts, actions and assumptions.

Listening is courageous. If we are truly listening we must always be prepared to change our minds, even on the most deeply held and treasured beliefs. Without that openness, others will quickly pick up our unwillingness to truly listen, even to the most challenging and unpalatable stories.

Listening well requires humanity. It requires creating a relaxed and comfortable environment. Fun must be part of listening. People are free to be open when their stories are not going to upset or destabilise the listener. We have to be prepared for inconsistencies, half-truths, and even downright lies! We will be tested, pushed, shock-tested, broken-hearted and appalled by what we may hear.

There was a woman who shared with me the story of her childhood of abuse, and early adulthood of drug use and crime. In some ways it was a typical story that I could have read in a newspaper or novel. Listening to her was a life-changing experience as it challenged me about how my life might impact this kind of story. It made me ask questions of myself – my own understanding, skills, courage, spiritual strength, theology. How might I work with others to make a difference to so many who have this same story, living together in networks of others who shared similar stories? What were their priorities? What did they really need? What did they value most? The answers to those questions were different to what I would have assumed. Where I looked at basic needs like food, housing and safety, they prioritised loyalty and forgetfulness. This story led me in new directions and continues to impassion me for the ministry I have given my life to.

We can easily imagine that others with different, often more horrific, life experiences to our own would not want to share their story with us. We imagine that we would need a similar journey to theirs for them to trust us. My experience has taught me that, valuable as it is to have come from the same culture and background, in the listening space the critical elements are acceptance and a sharing of humanity and pain. My husband, Mick, would say that when someone looks in your eyes and they see the cracks in your eyes, then they know you are OK. This is about having come to your own place of brokenness.

Jesus was a listener. To be a friend of prostitutes and sinners he certainly wasn't just preaching! He was also intuitive in his listening and saw through to the real issues people faced (John 4). That intuitive side is different to making assumptions and putting our own judgement on another. It is the capacity to listen to the Spirit and His insights while listening to the person. This takes many years of learning and some are more gifted at this than others. We should raise our intuitions as questions and not statements, test out what we think we see and be open to being wrong – it occurs more often than not!

I love to give advice. I take half a story and leap in my mind to the solutions. I love to fix and help. I love to be practical and tell others what they need to do. The trouble is that when I leap forward, others leap backwards and I get the solution wrong. I impose my own priorities and they know I haven't 'got' them. I see it in their eyes. 'Another do-gooder putting their own ideas out there and thinking they can change my community to make it what they would like it to be.' And they turn off. I have to pull myself back. Shut myself up. Open my ears and heart and take SO much more time. Be relaxed. Have fun. Be relentlessly curious. Hunt out the good with the bad. Point out the strengths and achievements of others. Hear what they most value. Acknowledge what they bring, and serve their dreams.

Jesus came that all may have life, and have it abundantly (John 10:10). May my listening lead to understanding of what real LIFE looks like to the other. May I hear the dreams and see the treasure when those dreams come to pass. May I listen to my own heart and understand what part is mine. May I understand what treasures I am being asked to bring to see the Kingdom of God here on earth.

Reflection

Listening is easy when you agree with what the speaker is saying but can be very difficult when we disagree or are being challenged or even offended. It requires us to focus on somebody other than ourselves. We must leave our own prejudices and assumptions at the door and be prepared to change our minds. It doesn't come naturally but we can learn to be better listeners.

Deliberately find someone with a completely different opinion or set of beliefs to yours and listen to them. Be open to having your own views changed. Be open to being wrong.

At the same time, listen to your personal reactions and hold them. Be aware of your head noise and hold it. Do not interrupt the other person, do not judge or argue. Raise your intuitions as questions. Do not try to change their viewpoint or give advice.

Listening in this way may lead you to discover something unexpected, to identify a need you didn't know was there, and to respond by doing something you never imagined. Dave Elston's story in the extras section is a good illustration of this.

Partner-
ships

Annie Kirke

In 2006, Annie started training to become a vicar in the Church of England and during this time was responsible for developing support work for homeless people and rough sleepers in London. In 2010 she began working as a Pioneer Priest in the Diocese of London seeking to support the emergence of missional communities: groups of Christians living life together according to the values of the Kingdom of God, sharing their lives and resources with those Christians and not-yet-Christians around them. She has remained a member of Westminster Churches Homelessness Task Force which opened its first winter shelter for rough sleepers this year.

City Lights Intro

When was the last time you felt hard done by? What did you want to be done about it? Where does your sense of justice come from? How do you feel when you see or hear about injustice?

In this piece, Annie Kirke looks at the idea of justice and our role when it comes to dealing with injustice.

T he Spirit of the Lord is on me,
because He has anointed me
to proclaim good news to the poor.
He has sent me to proclaim freedom for the prisoners
and recovery of sight for the blind,
to set the oppressed free,
to proclaim the year of the Lord's favour.

"Then he rolled up the scroll, gave it back to the attendant and sat down. The eyes of everyone in the synagogue were fastened on him. He began by saying to them, 'Today this scripture is fulfilled in your hearing.'" (Luke 4:16-21)

You probably could have heard a pin drop as Jesus sat back down after reading these long-awaited words from the scroll of Isaiah, in the synagogue in his home town.

Jesus had come to establish his Father's kingdom in our midst and this is what it looked like. It was about restoring beauty, hope and freedom to people, communities and nations.

What could it look like now?

Jesus came to reawaken people to the kingdom of God in their midst and to invite people to enter into it. To receive it. To become an agent of it.

From the minute we are able to communicate, concerns about whether or not something is 'fair' enter our conversations and relationships. I still remember getting smacked at playschool because I asked for a biscuit, only to watch another child take one and it be ignored. "But she just took one!" I exclaimed. "Don't be a tell-tale and go and sit down!" the lady in charge said. Hungry and confused, I discovered the girl who had taken a biscuit was her daughter. How did I know that it wasn't fair? I was only four!

We all carry a deep echo in our hearts for justice, of a world where we have a genuine concern and regard for one another, where we treat one another as we would like to be treated, where we consider one another's needs as well as our own. A place where everyone flourishes. But, in reality, our human experience can be quite the opposite!

In 2006 I started working at St Mary's Bryanston Square. I was responsible for developing our work amongst marginalised and vulnerable people. Several members of St Mary's had a real desire to serve the homeless so we began by mapping which churches and organisations were already working with the homeless in Westminster and seeing where there might be gaps or needs that we could respond to. ASLAN (at All Souls Langham Place) and the WLDC (West London Day Centre) were both working with homeless people, running meals and a drop in, offering specialist support. Both were looking for volunteers.

Over the course of a year, several members of St Mary's volunteered at both and we began to learn about homelessness and some of its root causes through relationship with rough sleepers and those that supported them. We also learned that The Church had a unique role in responding to the spiritual, emotional and physical needs of a person and how vital this is because they are all interconnected.

A year after we started, ASLAN wanted to start a second meal in another church because of their limited space. So in December 2009, a week before Christmas, we hosted our first homeless meal at St Mary's.

I've always been convinced that God has a deep love and compassionate regard for people who are marginalised and the meal confirmed it in so many ways. We prayed beforehand that guests would experience the tangible presence of God in our midst and that we would be able to share God's love with people in conversations and the way we treated them. One of the guests arrived and when he surveyed the room exclaimed, 'It looks and feels like heaven!' During the meal an investment banker who had moved

Each of us is born with an inher- ent desire to live a life of significance

to a house doors away from the church was on his way home from work and saw our homeless guests coming into the church. He stopped to ask what was happening and left his number asking for me to call him to discuss the meal. I have to confess I thought he was going to complain. Marylebone is a wealthy area and I expected some opposition to the meal. When I met up with him three days later he had lots of questions about the meal and what our intentions were. I explained we wanted to love people and help them move forward in their lives, that we hoped this would include finding accommodation and jobs, re-establishing relationships with loved ones and discovering their true worth and potential as individuals.

He donated £5,000 there and then to support the vision of the meals and has remained personally involved. One of the reasons the meal was successful was that we worked in partnership with ASLAN and the West London Day Centre. We didn't necessarily know who was a rough sleeper and who had a place to stay, but ASLAN and the WLDC did because they knew the rough sleepers by name. They distributed the invites for us and so we always had a rough idea of how many to cook for and who was coming. It also meant that if any issues came up with the guests, for example, needing to see a doctor or discuss a benefits claim, we could refer them back the WLDC for specialist support. Working together made us much more effective than if we'd worked in isolation and this was ultimately more helpful for the guests.

In November last year, Westminster Churches Homelessness Task Force (which I have joined) set up a winter shelter to provide a bed, warm meal and

friendship for rough-sleepers. The snow kicked in hard and fast and we knew that some of the guests at our meals would not survive on the streets. We approached the WLDC who agreed to assess and refer clients to our shelter. We started with four churches who were willing to host a night each. Once again I was impacted by God's compassion and love for the guests that we sheltered for seven weeks between January and March. We had some wonderful times talking and eating together, sharing life stories and hopes and dreams. God always felt palpably present. I think it was because we were doing what Jesus taught and did in the gospels.

Recently, we met to debrief, it was amazing to discover that over the course of seven weeks we'd sheltered thirty-five guests. Many had been re-housed in this time and some had gone for job interviews. We had provided practical, emotional and spiritual support for them for seven weeks and the benefit to their lives was real. I can't wait until next winter when seven churches plan on providing shelter from November to March. I know this will continue to grow and change lives because it is God's heart.

In Ephesians 2:10, Paul reminds the early church that they have been created to live extraordinary lives as followers of Jesus:

"We are God's handiwork, created in Christ Jesus to do good works, which God prepared in advance for us to do."

Paul makes several astounding claims. One is that you, right now, are God's workmanship, God's 'masterpiece'. The Greek word is 'poema' from which we derive the English word 'poem'. If Scripture is God-breathed, then, it is God who declares that you are God's poetry. Another claim is that you've been created to accomplish 'good' with your life. Each of us is born with an inherent desire to live a life of significance. To make a difference. To matter and to do things with our life that matter. To live a life less ordinary. We all do without exception.

Furthermore, you're the ideal person to do the 'good' that God made you for. And, whatever it is, that 'good' is as unique as you are.

Reflection

Annie quotes Ephesians 2:10 and says that you are the ideal person to do the 'good' that God made you to do.

What injustices are you aware of? How could you respond to these injustices? What are the gifts and abilities that you could bring to the table?

One of the reasons the homeless meals were so successful was that Annie and her team worked in partnership with ASLAN and the WLDC.

What relationships, partnerships or connections do you have that could be helpful? How can you invest in and develop these?

Saving the World is Dull

Mari Day-Revell

Mari grew up in Bristol. During her university years, she moved onto the Alton Estate in Roehampton, South West London, and became involved with Regenerate (www.regenerateuk.co.uk). In her early twenties, Mari moved to New Zealand for five years where, along with friends, she co-founded City Lights and worked for Iosis (www.isois.org.nz). Now back in London, Mari has gone on to co-found City Lights London with friends and is currently employed by Regenerate.

City Lights Intro

Intrinsic within us all is a desire to do something meaningful with our lives. This creates a tension when we also feel inadequate, too busy, daunted, uncertain, distracted, scared: the list goes on. Mari addresses these feelings in this piece through telling her story. In a nutshell, she deliberately exposed herself to need and responded by taking a risk. The greatest risk was facing her fear of failure. She started small. Her expectations did not line up with reality. It was a very difficult process but God ended up doing far more than she could have ever imagined.

E ver since I was a child I've had a sense that I was made for something bigger and greater than simply pleasing myself. Justice issues burn inside me. I vividly recall, when I was a teenager, hearing a man talk about his work with vulnerable children in the Bronx, New York. He told tragic stories about the sons and daughters of sex workers and substance abusers, and these kids were victims of abuse themselves. These stories became etched in my mind with a permanent marker and that day I remember saying a feeble prayer. I couldn't find words, it wasn't a clever prayer, more of an overwhelming desire to do something significant and meaningful with my life. I wanted to change the world or at least someone's world. I wanted to do something big. I didn't realise that often we must become the answers to our own prayers, otherwise we could spend our lives just waiting around for something to change. And if there's one thing I know about myself, I hate waiting!

Fast forward seven years. I found myself with the same feelings after meeting a twelve-year-old girl, whom I'll call Sasha, on the streets of Auckland, New Zealand. She was selling her young, underdeveloped body for sex.

Let me explain. In 2003, I volunteered for an organisation which offered support for street-based sex workers. We would venture out in a van during the early hours of the morning, handing out hot drinks and muffins! I felt so embarrassed handing out muffins. It seemed ridiculous to me and totally inadequate in the face of the chaotic and complex lives we encountered on those dark cold nights.

When I met Sasha it was about 1.30am. She got out of a punter's car and ran towards me. She immediately caught my attention, her young agile frame, beautiful unspoilt face and big brown eyes. She told me her story. I listened. Her father was in prison, her mother a substance abuser who that night had gone out to get a fix, leaving Sasha in the care of their neighbour. Her neighbour worked in prostitution and had taken Sasha out, training her to do the same. Sasha went on to tell me what the punter had made her do, just seconds ago, and how much he had paid her for it. Her neighbour and mentor took Sasha's face in her hands and said with excitement "See I told you, you would make a lot of money." I watched silently and felt a mixture of powerlessness and yet a desire to do something. Sasha's life disturbed me. She was so impressionable and vulnerable. I couldn't help but think that unless someone intervened, her life was about to set off on a track which might easily lead to devastation.

Sasha was my world, I wanted to do something to change it, but I did not see her again for a long time. She was, however, a catalyst in my life who led me on an astounding journey.

The impression of Sasha stayed with me so powerfully that I wrote her name on a piece of paper and stuck it on my wall. It simply read 'Sasha'. That might seem a strange thing to do and I had never done anything like that before, or done anything like it since. But this young girl had made her way into my heart and I wanted it to lead to something more. I never wanted to forget the way meeting her made me feel: I knew those strong emotions would propel me to action. I found out that Sasha represented hundreds of other underage girls in the sex industry.

I met more girls, heard more stories and started to understand these children were forced into this lifestyle by a lack of choices. I heard one girl say "I've been abused all my life, so I might as well get paid for it!"

Feeling totally unqualified, I nervously approached social services. I suggested we meet for a cup of tea because I had been meeting underage girls selling sex on the streets and I wanted to do some thing about it. I discovered that a group of concerned parties had been meeting for seven years about this issue, but nothing had yet been done. A large number of these girls were living

If you don't start small, you don't start at all

on the streets. When the police picked them up, they had nowhere safe to take them. One option was foster homes, but 'normal' family homes were not set up for the complexities of their needs, so the placements would inevitably break down. The other option was young offenders' units. So the felt need was emergency accommodation.

To a cut a long story short, together with an army of friends and with the backing of an organization called Iosis, we set up a home for these sexually traumatised children, which we called 'Awhina Teina', meaning 'to embrace the little sister' in Maori. It was a complicated and political journey but I saw the impossible happen. The unexplainable. A couple moved in to become the house parents and the vision of Awhina Teina became a reality: to provide the girls with options so they were not forced into prostitution. This experience birthed a belief in me that we must have a bias towards those who have been forced to the margins of society, often labelled and profoundly misunderstood.

By the time the home was up and running, I had moved in to live there as a support worker. I was naively ready to 'save' each girl one by one! However, nothing prepared me for the challenge of living there. Hard though those days were, I wouldn't trade them for the world, because the lessons I learnt were invaluable and incredibly formative for me.

I learnt that if I wanted to see transformation in communities or people groups, I must first be transformed myself by deliberately exposing myself to others' needs and engaging deeply with people. In other words, changing the world would begin with changing myself.

My friend Mick once told me "If you don't start small, you don't start at all." This reminded me of handing out muffins and the daily grind in Awhina Teina.

This 'changing the world' lark worked out differently from my expectations. Piles of dirty dishes every day, buying socks and new pyjamas for the girls, nagging them to do their duties, breaking up fights... I found myself feeling quite resentful while I was there. This wasn't how I had played it in my head. I felt trapped in the mundane, lonely and insecure. Perhaps some of the most important lessons are to be found in the dark places or in that pile of dirty dishes. Juggling the bigger picture with the small stuff is a tension that can be hard to live with.

And then there's the way that being alongside people who live in poverty forces you to face your own poverty. Poverty has many guises. In Awhina Teina, I was forced to go to the deeper, darker places in myself that I would rather avoid. In Awhina Teina, I was forced to address the hard questions in a way I never had to in the suburbs. Questions that I could so easily spend my life running away from.

A year and a half after I met Sasha on the streets, she was referred to Awhina Teina. She turned up on the doorstep and moved in at the age of thirteen. She has gone on to turn her life around. Of course it hasn't been straightforward – it never is – but she has shown remarkable courage. When I think about her, I feel convinced that although many girls were impacted through Awhina Teina, essentially it was all for Sasha. Nothing has demonstrated the love of God to me more powerfully than meeting Sasha and seeing what God did for her. These days, I have to remind myself never to get so caught up in the big picture that I lose sight of 'the one'.

Reflection

In a society obsessed with outcomes and results, Mari talks about redefining success. In light of this, take some time and consider these questions:

What is your definition of success and what is your definition of failure?

Are you so focussed on the outcome that you forget to find value in the journey?

Are you so focussed on success that you forget to see the value in failure?

Being proactive can feel overwhelming. Our resources feel inadequate in the face of great need. This is why Mari talks about 'the one'. Starting small is often the best place to start.

Can you identify one person, or one small area of need, which could become your focus?

Explore ways in which you can make a positive impact in this life or area. If it feels small, that might be a good thing.

A Life Exam- ined

James Odgers

James has been married to Henrietta for over twenty years and has four children. He started The Besom (www.besom. com) on his return from working for the first time with Jackie Pullinger in Hong Kong in 1987. It helps members of the local church to get out into the community around them and further afield amongst those in need. There are now over thirty Besoms across the country. He established FACE to Face in 1998 which helps single mothers from the African and Caribbean communities in South London who are on benefits or in low-paid work to start up a business, come off welfare and earn a livelihood. In 2002 he moved part-time to Somerset to establish a similar work with the rural poor (www.streamfarm.co.uk).

City Lights Intro

Exposing ourselves to needs, different cultures and different value systems can leave us feeling uncomfortable, because this will often challenge our own needs, culture and value systems. It is only when these are contested that we realise how important they are to us. Sometimes this might cause very strong emotions, like anger or fear.

"When we come face to face with the poor, it immediately turns around and rebounds on us!" James challenges us

to lead a life examined. This means going to 'the deep places', which many people would prefer to avoid; and deliberately exposing ourselves to 'the need' again. It means having honest and perhaps uncomfortable discussions with others and embarking on a sometimes painful process of increasing our self-awareness. Are you up for this challenge?

An interview with James Odgers

What is your definition of success?

My definition of success is learning how to love deeply, and then going out and loving and loving deeply, that's it. Everything else is completely secondary... It can only be done in relationships. It can only be done by experience: that's how God has always done it. He'll give us good relationships, bad relationships, easy relationships and hard relationships, some that we wish we had never got involved with and some that we long to have had more involvement in. There is no possible substitute for the sand in the oyster of a relationship.

> **My definition of success is learning how to love deeply, and then going out and loving deeply, that's it. Everything else is completely secondary... It can only be done in relationships**

What are some of the most common and challenging questions people have from their involvement with Besom?

The main questions all boil down to one, which is the great challenge for all of us I think: I have seen this, what shall I do? How do I live my life? How am I going to claim to be a Christ follower? This is always the case when we come face to face with the poor, it immediately turns around and rebounds on us.

Hopefully, the question will not just be 'Lord how shall I live now that I've seen the way that they live', but 'Lord how shall I live now that I've seen the way that you choose to live'. That's an even bigger question. It sharpens our response and takes us to the deep places we need to go to, if we're to have an examined life and a life that brings glory to God. Many people lead a life which is shallow. They hardly even begin to ask themselves the big questions and if they do - if the answer is going to lead to anything that might cause conflict, confrontation or change - then they'll just park the question and move on, rather than accepting it as a question that God has placed before them for this time.

For those people who do want to grow, develop and face those hard questions, can you advise how best to do that?

There are two ways: the first is theoretical and the second is practical. The theoretical way is, having been challenged, to find out what others who are wiser think about it. Your starting point will be Jesus of course, but then there

will be the experience of the saints through the ages. How did CT Studd decide to go to the Congo when he was about to be chosen to play cricket for England as he graduated from Cambridge? How could he have reached a place where he was about to turn his back on all that he knew? How do I deal with that? He has been a signpost for so many. Find out how other people have lived in the light of the questions that God has thrown up. 'How shall I live?' Mercilessly use those people who are a couple of miles further down the road and who are going to be able to tell you what that last couple of miles have been like.

The other way is deliberately to go into those places where we have been challenged, practically speaking. So if someone has been challenged by, say domestic violence, find out about it from others. There is a lot to find out, lots of amazing women who run refuges to talk to. The other way is to go back in and find out other ways of getting involved with those who are caught up in that sphere of abuse. Deliberately expose yourself to it again, but continue to work out with God why you feel like this. With The Besom, people often come back very angry about something. This can lead onto wonderful discussions. Anger that a single mum on the sixteenth floor of a council estate only had a big TV, but didn't have a bed for the child or anything in the kitchen. What a great starting point for a discussion. I mean that question goes everywhere, doesn't it?

Is it important to listen to your feelings?
Yes. It's a great starting point. In relation to the example above, why am I angry? Anger because I wish to impose my own value system here? What am I seeking to suggest? How do I know that that's an appropriate suggestion if I haven't had the experiences of being a single mum on the sixteenth floor? Of course if you are a single mum in debt and poverty on the sixteenth floor of a council estate, you can't afford a baby sitter and you probably don't dare go out much, certainly not after dark because the lifts are bound to be broken and the stairwells full of gangs, so what else do you do night after night after night if you don't have a TV?

So it's about embracing those really tough questions, rather than avoiding them?
Absolutely. And recognise that the little question has been presented to you, like a little nugget, from God. It is designed to encourage you to ask the bigger questions which aren't about them at all of course, they're about us, about my relationship with Jesus in the context that He's talked to us about.

What about people who feel like their contribution is pointless in the bigger picture?
Well if it feels too big, there's all the Mother Teresa language, an ocean made up of drops and so on. But I think a feeling of pointlessness often comes out of

somewhere else actually. I think more often it comes from a sense of inadequacy, rather than a sense of pointlessness. I think we often don't start because we are afraid that we've not got much to offer. So I think I would want quickly to move the conversation away from the pointlessness of the act to the feelings behind why one might use that sort of language.

When we come close to suffering, our understanding of God and faith can be rattled. What about those questions and challenges?

They need to be boiled down to something that is not a generalisation, start with that. So my response is: let's talk about specific circumstances of suffering and see whether we can get any light on those. The places of blessing that Jesus points us to in the Gospels are always places where people are grieving, dying, sad, diseased, lonely and suffering. In those places, we will meet with him, as Jesus says in Matthew 25, and with him we can begin to address it. But if we generalise, it can stop everything at any stage in our Christian journey. If he has chosen to be a lamp unto our feet (Psalm 119), we can always take the next step. That often seems to be all He's focused on. If we go forth and get involved with the appalling suffering, then when we look back we will see a very rich experience that we've had alongside a Jesus who knows and cares and loves everybody who is suffering.

When engaging with poverty, what is your understanding of evangelism in this context?

Great strides were taken in Lausanne in 1974, bringing the word, the spirit and social action together and recognising the fullness of the gospel in a way that had been seriously lacking. But I don't think that that is today's issue. I think today's issue is this: Jesus very clearly left us a new commandment before he left. He said this is how the world will know you are my disciples, if you love each other (John 13:35). The extraordinary business that we all love each other across every divide, gap and chasm is the greatest evangelistic thrust that we can possibly have, and it's been entirely overlooked. We followers of Jesus are as totally divided and separated as the world is. Thus we are ignored and we should be. I think this secret form of evangelism has been lost. Jesus does say 'go' in the great commission of course. But in the context that He's leaving them behind, he says 'love one another,' which we can only ever do on a small scale. Because how many real relationships of any depth and intimacy can we ever have in a lifetime? Not many. If you can really provide a bankrupt and desperate world with an example of love, which will be us loving each other with His love, then the world will beat a path to our door. That's evangelism.

How can we be effective in working with people facing issues like poverty in a way that empowers them rather than disempowers them?

We don't have a project, we don't have a programme, we're not there temporarily and we're probably not paid. We come alongside them, only because of the love that God has shown to us that we want to share. We come alongside them with a desire to build a relationship, not to draw people out of poverty, not to add them to a list of those who have come off benefits and not to add them to a list of people to whom we have provided a sofa. All we're ever called to do is to sow seeds. And the only way that we can do that is very slowly and carefully, and in relationship with those whom God has asked us to come alongside.

Reflection

Think of a time in your life when you were exposed to injustice. How did this make you feel? Remember that strong feelings often lead to deep discussions. Acknowledge the questions and feelings you were confronted with through these encounters. The chances are, these feelings will say more about you than anything or anyone else. They are worth exploring and discussing honestly if you want to increase self-awareness and respond to the challenge James gives us: to lead a life examined.

Action

James refers to people who are like signposts in our lives, those who are further along the track than we are. Can you identify any 'signposts' in your life, people with more experience than you who you can learn from? With an open mind, take your questions to one or two of these people and ask them for their perspective.

The Slow Revolution

Mick Duncan

Mick Duncan is a convert out of the hippie drug world, which therefore makes him now an older guy. He and Ruby have three children, two grandkids and no pets. They have lived and worked with local neighbourhoods and churches in NZ, Australia and the Philippines. In Manila they squatted in a slum and lived very simply. It was all a lot of fun and life-giving. Along with 'street degrees'', Mick has a few paper degrees in sociology and theology and has also written several books, none of them bestsellers! He is currently labouring away in yet another local neighbourhood with another local church. It is all hard work, but right!

City Lights Intro

In this piece, Mick encourages us to slow down: to be alert to ways we can show mercy and do justice in difficult situations; to physically sit or stand with those who are alone; to be friendship-orientated not goal-orientated; to remember peoples' names, especially those often overlooked and forgotten; to marshal ourselves, our resources and our strengths towards the weakest; to be willing to do the small things and to do what is in our power to do to influence change.

S o perhaps you have done a City Lights event or maybe you have started engaging with a need in your area. What next? There are no rules on this one but there is some wisdom. I think it has something to do with how we live. So I would like to suggest that from this point onwards we become slow activists who love mercy and do justice (Micah 6:8). The best way I can illustrate what I mean is to share some stories from my own life.

Doing 'Slow'

I had just come out of the hippie counter-culture; dirty hair to my ankles (a slight exaggeration), barefoot, wearing filthy clothes and still dazed from all the drugs. I was sitting in a church building, a one-week-old Christian waiting for the evening service to begin. On becoming a follower of Jesus I had followed up a recommendation to attend Spreydon Baptist Church in Christchurch, New Zealand. The hard wooden pew was uncomfortable and so was I. Looking around at 'the saints', I felt out of place and even a twinge of fear. What was I doing here? This was their place, not mine. They were the insiders and I was the outsider. To me these people looked odd. They were, as we hippies used to say, pretty 'straight'. I sat in the back row hugging my anonymity. I planned to do a runner and get out of there.

What I didn't realise until too late was that the pastor made it a practice to head toward the door as soon as his sermon was over. He casually sauntered down the aisle observing all as he went, and his eyes rested on me. We hippies were into slow and laid back but the pace of this guy was so gradual and measured it blew me away. I was impressed. He was what you might call a slow activist.

The pastor walked toward me, which can't have been an easy thing to do. Then he sat down. Sitting is a truly significant act. It communicates to the other that you are companionship-orientated and not goal-orientated. Never underestimate the power of parking your physical body next to another. I now look back on that moment as being the beginning of much of the healing I needed in my own life. No sooner had he sat down than came the inevitable awkwardness. We didn't know each other and we both were shy. He tried to engage. I simply stared at him and said nothing. The following Sunday the pattern repeated and this continued for weeks and months. Slowly I warmed to his presence and my ice-like demeanour started to melt. I didn't recognise it at the time, but I can now see he employed the art of sensitive enquiry.

He began by simply and gently enquiring where I was born, where I went to school and when it was that I had arrived in Christchurch. For weeks he probed for some foothold that would give him access to my life. It wasn't an intrusive or investigative approach but one that showed genuine interest.

I eventually told him I was born in Invercargill and after my parents separated when I was seven years old we had relocated. Hesitantly I began to unfold aspects of my life and dialogue gradually evolved. What did I think about my parents separating? He wanted to know about my mental traffic and so I revealed thoughts about all manner of events in my life. This art of sensitive enquiry spanned months.

About a month into this startling relationship, the pastor exclaimed, "Mick, how would it be if I now opened every door in my life to you?" I wondered what on earth he had in mind. Turned out he meant his kitchen door, his study door and he'd even answer his phone if I ever rang in the middle of the night.

Never take for granted the power of such promises. Such promises were the food of hope for me and for others who are broken and vulnerable. As Naomi's life unravels, it is Ruth who makes her a promise that she will stay with her even unto death. These promises spoke of options for the future and a better tomorrow; and became the source of great hope for Naomi. Ruth however becomes the one in difficulty and the ethnic minority (Ruth 1:22). Promises this time come from Boaz who offers work, water and protection. As with Naomi, these promises become the food of hope for Ruth. In a similar way when the Pastor at my church promised to open every door in his life to me, I was stunned but also filled with hope. Maybe my life could get better.

Doing Mercy

And my life did get better. In 1985, when I was about thirty and by then married with two little children, we left the shores of New Zealand and relocated to the Philippines - moving into the very heart of a slum. We were now missionaries. Now I am not suggesting that this be your next step but I want to share with you a story from our slum adventure that does point to what is next. It has to do with slow activists loving mercy and being willing to do the small things.

We will never forget our first Christmas Eve in the slum when were rudely awakened by the sound of rocks being thrown onto our flimsy corrugated iron roof. A gang of drunken men had decided to make our discomfort their entertainment. We huddled in a secure corner of our new home and quietly prayed for protection. I asked God if I might one day make personal contact with one of the gang members and see him come to Christ.

My opportunity came while I was toiling away learning the local language. Our method was to hit the streets and practice a few short sentences each day. One day I cornered two unsuspecting boys. "Ano ang mga pangalan ninyo?", I stammered, asking for their names. Fortunately they grasped my awkward attempts and I was informed one was Richard and the other Boyet. Once I'd exhausted my entire Filipino vocabulary, I simply stood my ground and smiled awkwardly. It seemed that neither the two boys nor this foot-shuffling, embarrassed New Zealander knew what to do next. All I could say was sige (okay) and walked off feeling very much like a two-year-old.

Two months later, while again labouring at language learning, I caught a glimpse of Richard about to turn into an alley. "Hi Richard", I yelled. He looked back with a mixture of shock and surprise before disappearing around the corner. Some months later there was a knock on our flimsy plywood door and there was Richard. Having gleaned a little more Filipino, I greeted him and asked what he wanted. "A bible study". "Come right on in", I replied, trying to contain a mixture of joy and humility.

Our time together was spent in literal bible studies. I pointed to an English verse and he located it in a Filipino Bible. For months we jumped back and forth learning from each other. Over this time I got to know Richard and his sad story. At the age of fifteen his parents split and deserted him and his six siblings. Forced to fend for themselves, they had made their home in a damp hole in the ground and Richard ran with a gang of thieves to feed his brothers and sisters.

We are to love mercy (Micah 6:8) and the least I could do, the only merciful thing I could think of, was to begin dropping bags of rice into this hole in the ground that Richard called home. It was in my power to do this (Proverbs 3:27). Over the decades this has become a rule of thumb for me: Step out, walk forward, and give a hand-out. If it's in your power then just do it.

One of the reasons I like the Parable of the Good Samaritan (Luke 10) is that it is as much about saying 'no' as it is about saying 'yes'. The Good Samaritan didn't take the bleeding man back to his house, nurse him back to health and set him up in a job. He was on his way to Jericho but did what was in his power to do at that time, which was to clean and bandage the wounded man, take him to an inn and pay for his overnight stay.

I continued dropping sacks of food for Richard and the starving bellies below. Some months later Richard came to me and blurted out, "I've become a follower of Jesus." I was shocked and surprised. "What did it for you?" I asked. For as long as I live, I will never forget his brief reply. "One day", he said, "you remembered my name." And that was it.

The poor are often the forgotten ones. No one remembers them, let alone their names. On the day I yelled out his name, Richard couldn't believe he had been remembered. He calculated that if the strange white missionary had remembered his name then possibly the God who sent the missionary family also knew his name. That led him down a path that to this day he is still travelling.

The former gang member who squatted in a damp hole in the ground and stole to feed his family had now made a genuine Christian commitment and we began to 'do life' together. Just as pastor Murray Robertson had poured his life into me, I got alongside Richard to disciple and mentor him. For years we met on a weekly basis and after a time, I began to wonder who was actually mentoring who. A real mutuality had crept into the relationship. All the while I continued to drop sacks of rice into his hole but with an increasing awareness that this mercy must morph into justice. Micah talks of loving mercy and doing justice.

Doing Justice

As Richard and I walked together I began to ask a new set of questions. There was a sense that I needed to get knee-deep in the real issues of his life, even if that meant rubbing up against some thorny challenges. Intuitively I framed four specific questions: I asked Richard to describe what was happening for him. I asked him to interpret why it was happening. My third question was more prescriptive: what should be happening for Richard? Finally, I asked, what did he think I should do for him? I didn't realise these questions were being asked by many others around the world who were also seeking justice for real people in difficult situations.

We are to marshal ourselves, our re-sources and strengths toward the weakest

These questions took months to answer. Eventually I came to see that Richard suffered from twin evils: lack of money and lack of land. Firstly, he had no money. There were no jobs for him to earn his way out of poverty and no cash to help him set up his own business. The neighbourhood loan shark's interest rates were exorbitant. Several banks outside the slum looked at me with disbelief when I enquired about loan facilities for the poor. They declared that the poor were not to be trusted and unlikely to repay any loan. I walked away unconvinced.

Richard was trapped. Even if he wanted to 'pull himself up by his boot straps,' he would first need boots and straps. The system didn't want anything to do with him. I came to understand something about the causes of social injustice. The laws of the land and the policies of government opposed him. The elite and the powerful had set up systems that favoured themselves. People like Richard were forced to the edges of society where they had little choice but to gather in the slums and live as squatters. They had been abandoned, isolated, discriminated against and forgotten. This was the reality of what had happened to Richard and why.

So what ought to be happening for Richard? I didn't just turn to the social sciences for answers but also to scripture. God created the earth for all to enjoy, not just the few at the top of the pile. The Israelites were clearly instructed

to make provision for those who had the least and have policies in place at the top of the cliff to ensure the poor were protected from injustice. Neglect of the poor incurred God's judgment. In Jesus, we see God on earth walking toward and coming alongside the broken, lame, hungry and the destitute. The Apostle Paul made his way around the Mediterranean world planting micro-communities of faith and instructing them to embrace the poor. Almost every page of the Bible speaks of a God who is for the poor, not against them.

I was left with one final question, what could I do for Richard? What power did I have to influence change in his life? I decided to do something that was way outside of my comfort zone. I would start up my own bank. After extensive research I put in play a rather simple plan. In each slum neighbourhood, sufficient sized loans would be awarded to the most feasible applications as decided on by a small community-minded committee. After a year or so, the repayment rate on all loans was ninety-five percent. So much for the negative forecast of the middle-class banking sector! Successful applicants further down the list would not receive their loans until those above them had repaid theirs. Ours was a revolving loan scheme. Repaid loans would become the seed money for the next batch of loans. Not surprisingly, everyone looked out for each other because it was in everyone's best interests that all the loans were repaid. Richard also got a loan and started a micro enterprise. At last he was earning his own money.

The second evil facing Richard, as a squatter, was land. Again I put myself on the line and joined an NGO (Non-Government Organisation) already active in the land struggle. Curiously, through the bank we had founded and other community projects, we had unexpectedly created a new political bloc in the slum. During the next elections we campaigned against the extreme right wing that wanted the existing system with all its corruption to continue. As an aligned person it seemed my life was now at risk. I was asked to make public speeches in support of our stand against corruption. At one meeting a neighbour began yelling that he was going home to get his pistol to shoot me. I recalled the incident where Jesus escaped through the crowd and I took this as biblical justification for doing a runner. The neighbour returned and shot someone else in the leg. To cut a very long story short, our bloc managed to win the day and the corrupt local politicians were ousted from power. This victory gave us a voice to try and persuade the National Government to grant land to Richard and his fellow squatters.

We unashamedly used our support structure within the community to influence the way people voted. We took sides. We sided with squatters against the landowners, the powerless against the powerful. Our actions upset the landowners and put local politicians out of office. While these people also deserve our love because all are stamped with the image of God, to say that everyone is equal does not imply that all must be treated equally. We are to marshal ourselves, our resources and strengths toward the weakest. The strongest are to be positively discriminated against in favour of the downtrodden. I did not hate the money lenders but I loathed the conditions they created. We attacked elitist capitalism but not the capitalist. We detested the corruption, not the politician. To take sides is not unloving but simply love changing its form. Love expressed as charity is about giving; but love expressed as justice is about taking from those who have too much.

Doing justice for Richard meant taking sides. This did not mean loving Richard and hating those who were creating the injustices. Hate is the opposite of love. What we expressed was anger with the corrupt oppressors. As 'alongsiders' we are called to be angry but not to sin in our anger. Our anger on behalf of another is to be righteous. I was angry about the cause of Richard's poverty, angry enough to start a bank and fight for land.

We are to love mercy but also do justice. Mercy for me was giving sacks of rice to Richard and his family. Justice, however, was taking sides and standing in solidarity with those who were being discriminated against.

Richard got his Bible College qualification, married and had children. In 1994 we sadly left Manila but I always wondered what would happen to Richard. A few years ago I received an email from him, sent from an internet café. He wanted to tell me that he was now a Methodist pastor and leader of a number of squatter churches. His grown up children are now all at college.

It all started with a simple prayer to Jesus while a gang was throwing rocks at the walls of our squatter home in the slums, a 'chance' encounter in an alley while learning the local language and an effort to remember a boy's name. It began with us coming alongside each other and a chance to express loving mercy. It continued with Richard becoming a Christ follower and a chance for me to do what was in my power to do in seeking justice. The story continues to unfold as Richard does for others what I did for him, and what Murray Robertson did for me.

Doing Scary
You may have read all of the above and thought that is way too scary for you. I can appreciate that. It was scary for me! But I want to write dangerous stories with my life. And the beautiful thing is that you can write these stories wherever you are. You don't have to go to another world or a slum but simply start in your existing world, be it your city, suburb or immediate neighbourhood. As you walk, slow down and see what is around you. Spot those people that sit or stand alone. Walk up to them and sit with them and if it happens that a conversation starts, jump into it and allow yourself to enjoy it. Over the weeks and months that follow keep an eye out for this person,

begin to do life with them and be alert to ways you can show mercy. As the relationship develops begin to ask the four questions and see where these take you. It is scary, and who knows what might happen. But then that's the fun of it - and let's be honest - most of us need more fun in our lives!

Reflection

Mick makes a distinction between justice and mercy. What do you consider to be acts of justice, and what are acts of mercy? Discuss this with friends.

Consider how your thinking has been challenged through the stories in this toolkit and ask yourself the question: 'Are there any changes I plan to make in my life as a result'?

Think about the four questions Mick posed to Richard.
• What is happening for you?
• Why is this happening?
• What should be happening?
• What do you think I should do for you?

Do you know any people in difficult situations, who are seeking justice? Can you get knee-deep in the real issues of their life by asking these four questions? It is easy to confine prayer to words, but consider this as a form of prayer.

Extras

Inside Out / Simon Gale

Louisa Knight's Story

Andy Smith's Story

Dave Elston's Story

Pauline & Adrian Hawkes' Story

Mark Yates' Story

Will Campbell-Clause's Story

Safe Practice Guidelines.

Inside Outside
Simon Gale

Let the inside of our church become the outside,
and the outside the inside.

Let the dreams rise up, some from the ashes, some from slumber to our surface.
Let the faith, and the memories it is built upon flow from the depths of our
beings out of our mouths and actions.
Let the healings, the restoration, the encounters with Jesus come from our
treasured hiding places to our vulnerable faces.

The inside become the outside.
The outside become the inside.

The lost, the struggling, the poor, our urban sprawls and city schools, the
talented kids who hid their art behind bedroom walls or along train tracks.
Outside become inside.

Our next door neighbour we've never seen, my hedonistic peers, more white
lines and bottled beers.
Our head teachers, our bakers, our candlestick makers, socialists and Tories
and environmental warlords.
Our outside we keep at arm's length. We need our arms breaking. Embrace
this world, this friend, this place, this sinner we pray for.
Let it make our hearts beat and minds think.
Let us close down our inward institutions and give birth to the vision, prepared
and moulded by Jesus.

The inside become the outside.
The outside become the inside.

Louisa Knight's Story

In 2007, Social Services referred a family to City Lights in Auckland. It was the first time this had happened and I was asked to take a team to visit them as part of the next City Lights day. I was co-leading a small group run out of an inner city church and I knew we had a great bunch of people who would be up to the task, so I gladly accepted.

I was forwarded an email from the social worker explaining the family's situation: a tired mother with seven kids including a newborn, a partially absent father and a sixteen-year-old daughter bearing many of the household responsibilities - all living in a council house in one of the poorest suburbs of South Auckland. The email continued by listing the other organisations involved: Child Youth and Families Services, Housing New Zealand and the Anglican Trust. Then it ended with 'What could you offer this family?'

The question was foremost in my mind when I first visited Leia. I made a mental list of all the 'things to do' as I walked into her house and we talked: bare kitchen cupboards, crayon scrawled over the walls, a broken gate her husband wouldn't fix and an old garden shed she was waiting for her husband to get rid of. The more we chatted, distracted throughout by four children vying for our attention, the less comfortable I felt about raising these as possible things my group could do. Even though the house seemed chaotic and sparsely furnished, it was still very much hers. Offering a new sofa and a group of Christians to paint her walls - when I didn't even know her yet – was that disrespectful? I suggested instead that we'd come over for a picnic, and I'd bring a friend who was a builder to talk about the shed.

So, five of us came with food, toys and cardboard boxes which we drew on and made forts out of with the kids. Leia and I talked some more. I also spent time with her teenage daughter. Our builder friend came and chatted with Leia's husband about his DIY plans. Seeing the men talk, I realised that fix-it help was a sensitive issue in this household, because he was very capable of doing it himself. To come in and 'do' without consultation would have been shameful and would have discredited him in front of his family. Later on we said our good-byes and as we drove off, we watched Leia's husband begin fixing the gate.

We promised them we'd come back on a Saturday each month for six months. Though we discussed 'practical assistance', for some reason it just never happened. We simply came, played, talked, shared food and spent time. Over time our relationship with the family grew and became more natural and easy. Still, I was frustrated. I wanted to leave some tangible evidence of our 'help', but no natural outlet for this showed up. Though, every time we returned the father had done new things on the property like create vegetable plots or built furniture.

At Christmas I turned up alone to drop off a hamper of food and presents to Leia. I knocked, the door opened, and the kids rushed passed out to the garden, leaving me standing on the doorstep. They were looking for all the others that usually came with me, who they thought had come to play. I left the hamper in the kitchen and noticed they had received another one from the Salvation Army.

The social worker asked 'What could we offer this family?' but my question was 'Who were we to this family?' One of our friends in the team was a health nurse and she chose not to return after our first visit. She said it was too difficult not to have her nurse hat on when she saw the kids. It was true we couldn't be their social workers, health workers or housing officers. Added to this, it was clear they were already in the catchment of several charitable organisations. I struggled with the tension of not being quite a social worker and not quite a normal friend. The lack of definition made it hard to know what was appropriate for us to do.

I unleashed this and other questions on City Lights leaders, church pastors and community workers. Some were helpful, others less so. Most just helped me word my questions better.

But a few answers did come during our visits. For example, one day Leia made treacle pudding for lunch. She exclaimed as she brought it out to the garden, that she had forgotten to make the custard. We all politely said it was fine and we didn't need it, except for one of our team who piped up that he'd LOVE some. So she went back and made a giant pot, pouring it out for us and her kids, and then insisting my friend take second helpings as we left. I know this guy, and imposing in that way was out of character. But he knew better than us that Leia should have opportunities to care for her guests and her children. That was one of the answers I came out with: take the custard, receive hospitality and wherever you can, empower others.

Andy Smith's Story

We moved into a housing estate in our early twenties. We were part of a small church group. We would meet on Thursday nights in our flat to chat and read the bible together.

At the same time, we were getting to know the estate. We noticed boarded-up shops, fights in the street, kids riding around on stolen mopeds without crash helmets. We saw violence in the pubs and drug dealing in the stairwells. After listening to local people, we heard and saw many more things in our community which were not good. There were many isolated elderly people with no gathering points, no family or friends; some hadn't been out of their flats for over twenty years. There were lots of young people with little to do and very few opportunities. There seemed to be very few positive role models. As we began to see and hear about these needs on our doorstep, we began to feel stirred. We wondered what could happen if there were positive role models for the kids, support for parents, and visits to the elderly.

As we listened to people living on the estate in Roehampton, we also listened to the desires within us, and to what we felt God was encouraging us to do. At the same time, we could see the opportunities and signs of hope. We began to dream about the changes that could take place if we responded to the needs and to the call on our lives to follow Jesus and practically live out our faith.

One of the things we did was sit down with a ten-year-old boy called Carl. He was getting himself into a great deal of trouble, and his life was not heading in a positive direction. We asked him what he and his friends would like to do. We got a piece of paper, a pen and he fired away. "Football, somewhere for us to hang out, trips" he said. We asked where he'd like to go on the trips. "Swimming, bowling, laser quest, the beach, skiing." We later found out that he meant ice skating, not skiing; he just couldn't remember what it was called.

Brilliant! You see, if Carl had said he wanted to go shark fishing or for flying lessons it would have been more challenging, but he said football and trips.

I love playing football! He said they wanted to play so we started our youth work with a football match. Simple! We got Carl to spread the word. We had no budget so used jumpers for goals. It was small. We played that first match in April 2000 and have carried it on every week since that day. Over 1,000 young people have been involved since then and many relationships have developed through it. But it started with about six lads on a patch of grass near where we lived. We also organised trips to the places Carl had said he wanted to go. These trips provided magic moments for these kids, memories that will last forever. Again, they were simple to do. We borrowed or hired a minibus, got permission from parents, charged a small amount of money and off we went.

Another example of our response to need was this. A girl in our small church group was a trained dancer. Some girls on the estate had said they wanted somewhere to go and were interested in dance. We matched the ability and the resources we had with the young girls' desire and set up a dance club once a week in a church hall. Significant relationships were formed in that church hall, relationships which remain today.

Alongside this youth work, we also set up a lunch club for pensioners. We started by leafleting some flats, inviting pensioners to join us for a coffee and to talk about the idea of setting up a lunch club. Twenty-three pensioners turned up and together we wrote a funding proposal, having set ourselves up as a registered charity. The council gave us some funding and it got going. One day a local guy, Grant, came to see me. He had heard that funding for the elderly was under threat. He believed that as a community we needed to value and respect the elderly. He wanted to throw a party for them where they would be treated like kings and queens. He was passionate about his vision and believed that even if the council decided the elderly on our estate were not a high priority, these elderly people still deserved love shown to them from within the estate. He pointed out that amongst us there were enough resources to do something ourselves.

We decided to throw a big party where elderly people could come for a free three-course meal, free drinks and entertainment. Grant used his contacts, a friend who worked at a local supermarket provided the food and another friend who worked for an events company provided tables and chairs. A lady who ran the local flower shop sorted out the décor and the rest of the money needed was collected from people in the local pubs. About two hundred elderly people turned up, some of whom hadn't been out of their homes for years! They were reunited with old friends, they ate, drank and had a great time. Some of the guests wrote afterwards to say it had been the best day of their lives. Local people – some of them well known to the police - waited on tables gave up their time to look after the elderly in their community. Every year since then, 'Kings and Queens' has been a growing event with even more people from the estate getting involved and helping. The local cab firm gives free lifts to and from the event and now over four hundred pensioners turn up with many more wanting tickets.

The football club, the dance club and 'Kings and Queens' all started small, with a dream and a desire to meet the needs around us and make a difference. From small things grow big things that have a huge impact in communities. Mother Teresa said, "Do small things but with great love" and Jesus said "The kingdom of God is like a mustard seed" (Matthew 13:31), the tiniest of seeds, but one which can grow and take up the whole garden.

Dave Elston's Story

I was looking for community and opportunities to love my neighbour when I sort of ended up living on a council estate by accident. I had a pretty low opinion of council estates – unpleasant and ugly places that should be torn down. Keeping an open mind one Monday night, I went to visit a potential flat on the Doddington estate in Battersea. I was blown away. Seeing the flat, being invited for dinner, meeting a dozen Christians all living in the tower block, and being prayed for, I was sold on the vision of Christian community, estate or no estate.

I got involved in the three-flat Christian community, which chiefly involved Monday nights eating and talking together. It quickly became clear that, whilst there was a general desire to get involved in social action in the wider community (and several ideas), little was being done. Feeling frustrated, my curiosity was stirred by an email about a prayer event on a nearby estate. It was encouraging that others in our part of town had the idea of building, investing and knowing our community! As a prayer group we became involved with London Citizens[1] and planned a Battersea-wide listening campaign. A listening campaign is a planned intentional action by a group of people to better understand the issues faced by those who live and work around us. It sounded a strange sort of exercise, but most of us thought it wouldn't do any harm.

One Saturday afternoon, we met with thirty others for some brief training before dispersing around several estates to listen to some local residents. In pairs we approached people: all sorts of people and people we wouldn't normally approach. After explaining who we were, we asked questions about how long people had lived there, how they find the area, whether there'd been any changes, what they like about the place and what one thing would make the area better.

Trying to listen rather than speak, we heard stories about a community of beautiful and diverse people, of improvements to the area, and intimidating youth who turned out to offer to carry the shopping. There were issues too: businesses struggling in the shadow of Tesco, boisterous young people appearing to have little to do, isolation and fear of going out after dark, and a locked rooftop garden that was hardly known about.

At the debrief we talked about the stories that seemed to resonate and stand out, and identified themes around a lack of community organisation,

[1] London Citizens is an alliance of churches, colleges, mosques, schools and charities that take action together for the common good of our communities. See www.londoncitizens.org.uk.

poor communication of events, safety and under-utilised green space. We were asked what made us passionate. Our themes boiled down to one action point, something doable. We had learnt about a garden on top of the community centre that was kept locked up. The residents' association secretary had mooted the idea of creating allotments, maintaining it properly and opening it up for local residents. We decided we'd arrange a meeting to speak with her to see whether things could change. We prayed and thanked God for this opportunity.

Several weeks later, while watching the football in a local Ghanaian restaurant, we found ourselves discussing the garden with a local lady. She turned out to be the secretary we'd been trying to meet. She was sure that nobody wanted to use the space with Battersea Park so close, and she was anxious about the potential for drugs, fire, general mess and the lack of community ownership. We took a look at the garden, but we'd reached a stalemate.

Then out of the blue, posters started to appear around the estate advertising a gardening club meeting. The residents' association had the opportunity to set up a community garden and needed people to organise the upkeep, supervision and use of it. A few of us from the Doddington went to the meetings and almost by default I found myself being handed keys to the garden by the council. Suddenly we were responsible for the secret rooftop garden, yet none of us were even gardeners!

We were given a substantial grant from a local residents' association to buy tools and plants and there was an upcoming City Lights event scheduled. It seemed the perfect opportunity to launch the garden, with lots of volunteers available to help. Many families from the estate came up for the first time and helped clear out stacks of debris, put up a shed, suggested a name and did some planting. We started opening the garden every Saturday morning and formed a particularly close relationship with two guys who also helped run the residents' association. Different people have come together from all over the estate.

In six short months God unlocked the gate to a garden we didn't even know about and gave us the opportunity to come together with our neighbours. When we took the time to listen.

Pauline and Adrian Hawkes' Story

It was a sad occasion as Pauline and I visited our friend Alan in hospital. We knew he was very ill and dying. While we were there he turned to us and said, "You need to be helping refugees." When we asked what he meant, he replied, "You just need to do something about them." I guess we both saw this as some kind of prophetic word. The problem with prophecy is that you don't always know how to react or what to do, and at that time we didn't!

A few weeks later we saw in the news that a Norwegian boat had picked up refugees in the sea off the coast of Australia and tried to help them land. They were rescued from almost drowning. It must be awful to risk your life escaping from your home and all you know, to go to an unknown land. The Prime Minister of Australia refused to allow the people to disembark, and I think some of them subsequently died. Pauline wanted to catch a plane and punch the Prime Minister for his inhumanity and lack of human concern[2].

As a couple we had fostered around thirty children for the local authority for some fifteen years. We had wondered what we should do with that experience, and the news programme became a sort of catalyst. While Pauline was jumping up and down, I was trying to defuse the situation and protect our TV from being attacked. I said "Pauline, there are many refugees in the UK in need, why don't you start here?" I suggested phoning Social Services, because they knew us and maybe they already had some kind of refugee department.

Pauline asked whether they had a department dealing with refugees. They put her through to the manager of the department, and it turned out that Pauline and this man had worked together before, delivering training to the local authority's foster carers. He told her about the need in the area and explained that now he was the manager of the authority's refugee department. He was very grateful for anything we could do to help.

We discovered that the local Muslim community had already 'stepped up to the plate' and were meeting many needs by providing homes. We asked them for help and advice as to how to start and what was needed. We ended up learning much from their expertise. We were somewhat saddened that there seemed to be no Christians doing anything to help. For that reason, we did not come with a 'Christian' agenda or a church-based view. Rather we came as willing helpers from a company we set up, called Phoenix Community Care.

We decided that our help had to be centred round providing accommodation. Our daughter Carla, her husband, three boys and extended family decorated

2. The 2001 'Tampa Affair'

their house and moved out, allowing us to use their property to house refugees. There were months of preparations and huge costs. Bureaucratic regulations often make it very hard to help or do any good. Yet today we have some ten houses and can accommodate over thirty people.

We are still good friends with our first ever client. The process works like this. Social Services call our company saying that they have a person we can help. If we have space we arrange to collect them, usually from a Social Services office, or occasionally a police station. The first time Pauline went herself. When she arrived, the social worker pointed to a young lady crouched in a chair, holding a plastic bag and looking extremely drained. Having being introduced, Pauline drove the young lady to the house. We try to make the accommodation as nice and welcoming as possible. We call it the 'wow factor'. Pauline showed the young lady the rooms and food, and let her choose any room, because she was our first guest. The young lady chose and asked if she might sleep. She climbed into bed, coat and all, and dropped into a deep sleep.

Pauline then drove the car around the corner, parked, sat and had a cry. She was shocked by the terrible situation that these people find themselves in. She then phoned me at home and said, "Get me another house quick - we need to be helping these people!"

We have expanded since those early days. We not only accommodate these young people, but we also have our own foster care agency. This was initially conceived because although the refugees we dealt with were sixteen years old and more, many who find their way to the UK are much younger. We also formed another company, the London Training Consortium, to deal with education needs, and particularly ESOL (speaking English as a second language).

There is still a great need for help in this area, despite the government trying to discourage refugees from entering the UK. As we watch the news and see the wars and dangers that people are in, we see that people are going to run somewhere and some will make it to the UK. Often we can tell by where our clients come from where the latest 'hot spot' or war area is.

Incidentally, we did not announce that underneath it all we have the love of Christ motivating us. Nevertheless, Social Services did latch onto the fact that we were 'followers of the way.' They have often said of Phoenix Community Care and its placements that our 'people seem to go the extra mile.' This seems like a good biblical principle and Matthew 5:41 comes to mind. We hope this will always remain the case.

Mark Yates' Story

My name is Mark Yates, and I manage a project called LA-UK on behalf of Spurgeons. I have worked on the project for eight-and-a-half years.

The first thing that pops into my head is that the London marathon is twenty-six miles long – and you complete it step by step. The marathon analogy is interesting to reflect on because our culture puts a lot of emphasis on success and results right here, right now! We live in an instant coffee world. I boil the kettle, put a spoon of coffee in a jar and it's done. But someone had to work the fields, grow the crop, pick the coffee beans, grind the coffee beans, put it in a jar, stack it in a container, fly it to our country, unpack it at the supermarket and stack it on a shelf. I do an online shop and some 'fella' wheels it up to my door. I put the jar of coffee in the kitchen and boom – that's it – an instant coffee world. We never consider the process, we just want the finished product.

But what is the finished product of a human life? How do we measure that? Am I a finished product? No! Then what gives me the right to label a young person 'NOT a finished product'? Many funders want a finished product – they want a nicely packed jar of coffee to match the cost of their investment - but life is not like that.

Going back to the marathon, you might look back after three years or ten years and your organisation may or may not have won various awards. You may or may not have told your story in a book and sold a million copies. You may or may not have the ear of governments. Those things (if they happen) might be good, but basically our job is putting one foot in front of another, one step at a time. Sometimes we're running, sometimes we're taking pigeon steps: either way we're finishing the race put before us, one step at a time.

If I was commissioned to write an 'idiot's guide' I would probably say:

- Keep it simple.
- Have a team.
- Have a 'counsellor' figure in your life
- Be a significant adult.

In early 2000, I started walking the streets of the Alton Estate in Roehampton. There is a massive green so I borrowed some portable five-a-side football goals and bought a ball – and off we go. The kids just came and played football. Simplicity. That's one thing I've learnt in all these years.

Secondly, team is really important. If you're independent then give up. You need a team. Passion: well passion is infectious.

Thirdly, I am often there to listen to the children, young people and families as they unload issues, disappointments and frustrations. Encourage them in their work. So what about you? The leader or manager also needs a 'counsellor' to unload on.

Finally, be a significant adult. It doesn't matter what your skill is. Arts, dance, drama, music, skating, basketball or DJing. Children and young people will be drawn to that and you can be a significant adult in their life. Significant.

The phrase 'The Accompanist' is stuck in my head. Imagine you're at the cinema, and in the background an orchestra accompanies the film. You're not really conscious of it because you're watching the film. Although the music affects the scenes you're viewing, it is mostly a subconscious thing. A significant adult can be like the orchestra accompanying the journey of a young person. I am not there to tell them what they can or cannot do. I'm not there to save them. I'm not there to fix them. Those are some strong lessons I've learnt in the last two years. I am there to accompany them on their journey. 'Accompanying' makes me think of the birds singing. When was the last time I stopped and listened to their song? Behind the noise of traffic, and the noise of life, and the noise of the street and the noise of a fresh Facebook status update, the birdsong is accompanying all this in our subconscious.

How LA-UK Began

The WIRE Project in Littlehampton closed down in March 2007. I had been working for Spurgeons at the WIRE since October 2002 as a youth worker and project manager. The funding had finally dried up. The positive thing was that many of the clubs we had been running had been taken over by local churches and youth clubs. Due to the new Children's and Families Centre in the area, built in 2005, the community actually had more activities and quality provision than ever before, in the heart of an area which has remained around the bottom ten percent on the Index of Multiple Deprivation over the last twenty years.

In March 2007, in the space of five days, I was given around £120,000 from five different donors with a consistent message: re-brand and re-launch. The council gave me the 'top fifty' young people who particularly needed further support. I then topped this up by adding thirty young whom I knew of from my previous work in the community.

Keeping it simple: I selected the one and only service from the work of the WIRE (a group called 'The CREW') which no other agency had picked up on, and I revamped it. I launched 6 groups for different ages and bought a minibus. We ring the young people after school to check that they're coming. We then collect them in the minibus. We take them away from school and from where they live, to have a fun few hours of activity: on the beach, in the woods, building fires, toasting marshmallows, ice-skating, bowling, swimming, cooking, going to the cinema and so on.

At the time of writing we run three groups and also do 'one-to-ones' with individuals who need a listening ear and further support, referred to us by senior staff in schools or from social workers and education welfare officers.

Will Campbell-Clause's Story

In September 2008 a small group of us moved to an estate in Camberwell. Our vision was to be a community who worshipped God together, where each person was known and loved, where we shared what we had with one another, and where we sought to serve other residents of the estate in ways that God inspired in us.

We committed ourselves to two 'house nights' per week, in which we prayed and worshipped together, sought to be as open as possible with one another and prayed for each other. Initially three of us were in unpaid work and one person worked to earn enough to cover our rent and bills. Food and other expenses needed to be prayed in and we saw God's goodness time and again as we trusted in Him for this.

To discern what God was doing, we needed time on the estate to get to know people, and to sense what God wanted us to join in with. Some of us left our jobs or took up part-time work so that we had time to spend praying, meeting people and looking around.

During this time, we felt that God was connecting us to some key people on the estate. After a meeting with the chair and secretary of the tenants' and residents' association, we realised that joining the association would help us to be more part of the community. This was the first step for us, as we then felt more accepted and we were told 'whatever you want to do, we'll support you' – which felt like it had God's grace all over it! We started to dream about gardens springing up, vegetable-growing, compost bins, and people coming together through communal gardening. It was exciting, but required patience to let things build slowly.

In February 2009, a large area of land was left derelict when builders who had been using it for their site office, departed. The site was a focal part of the estate and had huge potential to be transformed into a community garden, so we did a petition among local residents about this idea. This happened to coincide with some council grants being offered to community groups to make unused spaces cleaner, greener and safer. On the back of great support for the community garden idea, we successfully applied to the council for funding.

With this funding, we have begun transforming the site into a beautiful orchard with raised beds for vegetable growing. As this is public land, the work has to be done by contractors, but we have to involve people as much as possible for the sake of local commitment to the project and local ownership of the project. The community tree-planting in 2010 was our highlight.

The work has not all gone smoothly, and there is a daily need to refocus on God's timing. The bigger the project and the more useful the land is for other purposes – for example this could have been a site for building new flats – the harder it is to get the permissions required. Because of the time lags and bureaucracy in meeting these requirements we turned our attention to the rest of the estate, where derelict spaces abounded.

We were keen to grow our own vegetables as much as possible, but when we started trying to do this, we found that a great number of residents had mixed feelings about what we were up to. Some loved it: guerrilla gardening was just becoming fashionable! But others said it would get trashed so there was no point. It was interesting to us that none of what we planted was wrecked, and people were even very restrained in taking veg from the very public growing site. It was great that others began to join us and we made many new friends and learned so much about gardening from many different cultures and traditions. One of our friends planted up her whole garden with salad, tomatoes, and peppers and she lived off it for the summer!

This vegetable growing took off, and we then started a gardening club on the estate. We worked on pensioners' gardens, planted vegetables in various patches and encouraged others to join us. It was good fun and we met more people, although we were shocked how many people just wanted to get all plants out of their gardens forever! Our early efforts at the garden club didn't attract many others who were keen to join in, but it was good in that people saw we were keen to help and they knew we cared enough about the area and the people to get active.

While we were seeking more funds to complete the big garden site, one of the funds we came across was perfect for the gardening club. So we applied and after a long wait and more bureaucratic process we managed to get a local environmental charity in to run the club. They brought in gardening expertise and experience in community work, which was sorely needed to make a long-lasting impact on the estate. As a result the garden club has now become part of the life of the community and has a regular group of attendees.

Looking back, it's clear that the key to it all was prayer. Additionally, waiting for the right time and meeting the right people was fundamental to enabling this to take off. Being a part of the tenants' and residents' association was significant because it allowed us to work with the community as part of an existing recognised group.

The organisation A Rocha UK (www.arocha.org.uk) have supported and encouraged the project from the start.

City Light's Safe Practice Guidelines

Looking after yourself

- If you are working on your own, always tell someone where you are going.
- Work in pairs if you are unfamiliar with a situation or if there is any uneasiness.
- Do not spend time in isolation with the opposite sex – always work in pairs.
- Do not go in to anyone's bedroom.
- If you sense any threat of danger, get out of the situation.
- Avoid burnout by setting and communicating appropriate boundaries, and by working effectively with others. The volunteer's role is to empower rather than create dependency.

Safe Practice when working with children

- Ensure you are not in isolation with a child - it is always best to work in pairs.
- Do not go into a child's bedroom.
- Do not take a child to the toilet on your own. Work in pairs. Monitor physical contact (especially if the child is particularly clingy) – side hugs are more appropriate than full frontal hugs. Finding healthy alternatives are important so the child doesn't feel rejected.
- Avoid play fighting.
- If a child discloses any information to you which causes concern about their welfare, write down what the child has said (word for word) and pass this on immediately to the project leader. Do not ask the child questions and do not discuss what the child has told you with anyone else, including their parents. These are legal requirements.
- Remember your role is a friend or mentor to the child. Therefore, avoid becoming a counsellor or social worker. Keep your role clear and simple to avoid complication.
- Do not advocate smacking or physical discipline and do not smack children or use any form of physical discipline. Do not talk to the children about other children or your colleagues. We need to show the children that we respect people's privacy.
- If you witness anything that causes concern, please inform City Lights.

Confidentiality

We have been given an opportunity to interact with many of the people we work with, and have built up trusted relationships with different agencies. It is our responsibility to protect and maintain their privacy. You are required at all times to keep information such as names, addresses and family situations confidential. The only exception to this is when you must report suspected abuse to a trusted third party, such as your project leader. Do not communicate with the press or other publicity media about any individual or family.

You must also never take photos or video of any of your projects without first clearing it with your project leader. If you are allowed to take photos or videos you must not make them public under any circumstances, including posting them on Facebook, Twitter or other internet sites.

Giving

If you want to give anything to a family please do not do so without permission first from a City Lights leader. If any specific needs are drawn to your attention please let us know.

You must not supply alcohol or cigarettes to any person you are in contact with through City Lights or during your volunteer time.

Transportation

If you are required to transport adults or children as part of your volunteer activities, please ensure that:
You have informed your team leader or City Lights key contact.

- Your car has a current MOT, up to date tax disc and insurance.
- The driver is licensed and fit to drive.
- You drive within the speed limit.
- You do not overcrowd your car: every person must have their own seat.
- When transporting children that you have approved car seats which are appropriately sized and fitted correctly.

Being sensitive

Reciprocal hospitality: hospitality is an important aspect of building relationship in many cultures, so it is wonderful to respond with acceptance and participation wherever possible.

As volunteers our primary goals are to build relationships, meet needs and empower individuals. Sharing your faith may prove to be a natural and loving part of this journey, but could work against your primary goals if it comes as a forced and one-way delivery.

City Lights works with people from a variety of cultures and religious persuasions and we ask that you are respectful of all cultures and religions.

Faith and prayer
We encourage you make prayer central to what you do (not necessarily publically).

We feel it is important to remind ourselves that we will not see the outcomes for so much of what we do in life, but we work in faith, and faith is not what is seen but what is unseen.

Expectations of Volunteers
We would encourage all volunteers to develop relationships in the community when your involvement with City Lights has finished, though this is not essential and there is no pressure for this to happen. Please inform us if you are planning to see families or individuals again. We also encourage everyone to start small and slowly, and not to overcommit themselves. We would rather your role is less frequent and consistent than frequent and unsustainable. We suggest a once-a-month visit until you are able to establish a stable relationship with families or individuals and with good communication in place. After that you may want to move to more frequent and casual contact with the families or individuals.